The Power of
THE HSTs

In autumn 2005 two 2+8 HST sets were leased by Porterbrook Leasing to Cotswold Rail, for charter and spot-hire use. As part of the deal, power car No. 43070 was re-liveried into Cotswold Rail silver and No. 43087 was branded into a Hornby model railways red and yellow colour scheme. The re-livery work, using vinyl, was undertaken at Tyseley depot, where the pair, complete with a buffet car also in Cotswold silver, are seen on 10 November 2005. *Wilf Smith*

Sporting the original version of First Great Western livery, with white cab body sides and side swirl, No 43032 *The Royal Regiment of Wales* leads the 08.45 Paddington-Penzance service past Langstone Rock near Dawlish Warren on 12 July 2003. *CJM*

The Power of
THE HSTs

Colin J. Marsden

An imprint of
Ian Allan Publishing

Contents

First published 2006

ISBN (10) 0 86093 600 7
ISBN (13) 978 0 86093 600 8

© Ian Allan Publishing Ltd 2006

Published by Oxford Publishing Co

an imprint of Ian Allan Publishing Ltd, Hersham, Surrey KT12 4RG.
Printed by Ian Allan Printing Ltd, Hersham, Surrey KT12 4RG.

Code: 0604/B

Visit the Ian Allan Publishing website at www.ianallanpublishing.com

Foreword

Some 30 years after it was first introduced, I am proud to say that the High Speed Train (HST) remains the workhorse of the inter-city operation in the Western region, and still performs vital services on both the East Coast and Midland main lines.

The introduction of HSTs into regular service in the late 1970s revitalised inter-city travel with the customer experience and use of railways being transformed.

The two lasting memories I have of my first journey on an HST are firstly the then bright orange and blue upholstery, which was completely different from any other train in operation at that time, and the smoothness of the ride. Even today, hardly a week passes without a customer commenting to me how much they enjoy the comfort, ride quality and general ambience of the HST. This is testament to the vision of the designers and the expertise of the engineers who developed and built this marvellous train; a train which still competes with advancements in automobile technology, as it whisks customers to their destination at speeds of up to 125mph.

This book illustrates a number of the subtle changes that have been made to the HST formation in the early years. These include the introduction of two refreshment vehicles on East Coast services prior to electrification and the introduction of the TGS coach. The livery changed during British Rail times and privatisation has brought further significant variety in liveries. But, like a supermodel's face, the HST takes each new guise well, always looking stylish and contemporary.

As a daily traveller on HSTs, I look forward to more years of enjoyment with further improvements to reliability being made by today's hardworking and dedicated maintenance crews. However, as we look to the future, I truly hope that the specifiers, designers and engineers involved in the replacement for our beloved HST create an alternative of such high quality that we are happy to bid farewell to this very special train.

Alison Forster
Managing Director
First Great Western

Title Page: Broadside view of First Great Western-operated No 43125, showing the revised livery without the white cabside, perhaps looking smarter in overall appearance. *CJM*

Right: In traditional CrossCountry formation, marshalled with just one first class vehicle shown here coupled behind the leading power car, the 17.10 Plymouth to Leeds service pulls round the tight curve at Aller divergence, west of Newton Abbot, on 19 July 2002 with power car No 43064 leading. With the driver's cab side door propped open, it was likely that the cab air-conditioning was not working correctly, a frequent problem with these vehicles in later years. *CJM*

Introduction

Welcome to *Power of the HSTs*. It hardly seems possible that it is well over 30 years ago that I became one of the first passengers to sample high-speed train travel in the UK, when I was one of the invited guests on board the prototype HST set undergoing tests on the East Coast main line. Thankfully I was also one of the first passengers to travel on the same set during the course of passenger trials on the Western Region, and one of the first to take advantage of a then British Rail Western Region offer to travel on an IC125 for just £1.25 in the weeks leading up to squadron passenger service.

Much has happened to the HST fleet in the intervening years. The interiors we see today, while based on the original design, are largely different and reflect the current passenger demands. Few external changes have been made to the fleet and the iconic design of the trainset is as timeless as the profile of Concorde is to the air industry.

Although much is speculated about the replacement for the HST, or HST2 as it has become known, the HST we see today will hopefully be around for many years to come — its passenger comforts are unequalled and, as many present train operators have found, the development of other multiple-unit-based express sets have not been anywhere near as successful.

By far the largest operator of the HST fleet is FirstGroup, operating the majority of its Greater Western Franchise services with the stock. New franchise commitments issued towards the end of 2005 will see more development of the HST fleet in terms of improvements to the passenger environment as well as technical changes, including re-engining with the latest technology.

Authoring *Power of the HSTs* has given me great pleasure. In searching out a wide and varied collection of illustrations of the fleet at work and rest, I have been struck by the diversity of liveries brought about by the privatised railway network. Nobody can ever say our railways are drab and dismal.

I hope you enjoy browsing this title and reading about what is, without doubt, the world's most successful diesel train, and long may it remain in front-line passenger service.

Colin J. Marsden
Dawlish
February 2006

The Prototype Train

Above: After assembly at the BREL Workshops in Crewe, the two prototype train power cars, Nos 41001 and 41002, were transferred to the Advanced Vehicles Laboratory at the Railway Technical Centre, Derby for static and dynamic testing. While at Derby, the vehicles were married up for the first time with the Mk3 passenger stock, built at the BREL Derby Litchurch Lane plant. Power car No 41001 is seen inside the Advanced Vehicles Laboratory soon after arrival from Crewe in June 1972. *Author's Collection*

Below: On 31 July 1973, just prior to introduction on East Coast services on a trial basis, the 2+7 prototype set, led by power car No 41002, is seen south of Peterborough on a trial and staff training run. At this stage the formation had two refreshment vehicles, one for first class and one for standard class passengers. The first class car is formed as the second passenger coach. *P. H. Wells*

Above: By the time this illustration was taken on 27 September 1975, the prototype HST was reclassified as 252 and allocated the multiple unit set No 252001. The distinctive train, clearly showing the power of the centre headlight, approaches York with a VIP special from King's Cross to celebrate the official opening of the National Railway Museum. *B. Watkins*

Below: The first day that passengers on the Western Region could sample high speed rail travel, and the comforts that it was to bring, was on 5 May 1975, when the prototype set was introduced on two return trips on the Bristol-Paddington route. On the first day of operation the set emerges from Box Tunnel, bound for Bristol. *George Heiron*

Left: The prototype HST No 252001 departs from Bristol Temple Meads and heads for Weston-super-Mare on 29 May 1975, when HST travel in the UK was less than a month old. At this time the train was operating just two return services between Weston-super-Mare/Bristol each day, working at a maximum speed of 100mph, as at the time route clearance for 125mph running had not been given.
Graham F. Scott-Lowe

Below: Looking its most majestic in 'reverse Pullman' colours of light grey body with a blue band and yellow warning end, the prototype set No 252001 passes Tilehurst near Reading on 7 April 1976 with a high speed test run from Bristol Parkway to London.
David Canning

Above: In connection with 'Stockton & Darlington 150' events held in September 1975, the prototype HST set was used to show off the next generation of rail travel. On 27 September the set was used to convey His Royal Highness the Duke of Edinburgh to Eaglescliffe to attend celebrations in nearby Preston Park. After forming the Royal Train, the set is seen entering Stockton. On the left is Class 31 No 31319 with an 'up' empty van train. *Ian S. Carr*

Right: The first fare-paying passengers to travel in a HST made rail history on 5 May 1975, when a huge celebration surrounded the departure of the 07.45 Bristol Parkway-Paddington via Chippenham service. It was the first official HST passenger train in the UK, as prior to this all trains formed of the Class 252 had been demonstration or press specials. The train is seen passing Stapleton Road on the outskirts of Bristol. *Philip Fowler*

Design, Build and Introduction

Above: Even while the prototype HST was under early assembly, drawings and models of a production High Speed Diesel Train were emerging. The now-familiar structural design is clear in this model shown at a trade exhibition in 1975. *Author's Collection*

Left: Assembly of all HST power cars was undertaken by British Rail Engineering Ltd at their Crewe factory, with usually around 10 vehicles under fabrication and construction at one time. On 6 April 1982, power car No 43191 receives final body filling and preparation before painting. *CJM*

Right: In the mid-1970s it became a regular sight to see HST power cars operating back-to-back between Crewe and Shrewsbury, sometimes in an unpainted state. These light power moves were to provide dynamic testing as part of the rigorous pre-delivery test programme. On 15 April 1976, Nos 43013/015 pass an all-over BR blue-liveried Class 101 DMU set at Shrewsbury as they arrive from Crewe. *I. Dewar*

Below: Huge celebrations surrounded the completion and delivery of the first production HST power car, No 43002, which although completed in 1975 and shown at the works open day in September, was not delivered to the Western Region until early 1976. Sporting a black upper-body band, the first production HST power car is seen in the works yard at Crewe in this posed view. *BREL*

253 039

Above: On 5 June 1980, set No 253035, formed with power cars Nos 43139/140, emerges from the 209yd-long Kennaway Tunnel and approaches Dawlish with the 05.07 Penzance-Paddington 'Golden Hind' Pullman service. At this time semaphore signalling still existed in the West Country, not being replaced by colour light signals until the mid-1980s. *CJM*

Left: Set No 253039, formed with power cars Nos 43147/148, starts the final descent into Plymouth as it crests the incline at Hemerdon on 26 June 1981 with the 08.25 Paddington-Plymouth service. *CJM*

Right: The Cotswold line saw the introduction of HSTs from 14 May 1984, with the 10.25 Paddington-Great Malvern and 13.43 return formed of HST stock. On 11 July 1984 the London Paddington-bound service passes Finstock station, formed with power cars Nos 43010/019. *Paul A. Biggs*

Above: A full West of England HST service was introduced from May 1980, but members had been used on many services prior to that date. Introduction on the Penzance-Paddington route allowed a 5hr end-to-end journey to be introduced. On 17 June 1980, power car No 43121, originally built as a 'spare' car, powers the 13.45 Penzance-Paddington past Burngullow, near St Austell. *CJM*

Left: In its proper formation with two first class passenger carriages at the London end of the train, set No 253013, led by power car No 43026, traverses the up main line at Twyford on 29 July 1978 forming the 12.45 Bristol Temple Meads-Paddington service. *CJM*

Above: Passing the Dawlish down home semaphore signal, HST set No 253022 slows for a station stop at Dawlish with the 08.35 Paddington-Paignton service on 14 June 1984. By the lack of people walking along the sea wall the weather, while bright, may not have been very warm. *CJM*

Below: Taken from where the M25 motorway now crosses the Great Western main line just the London side of Iver station, HST set No 253026 heads west on 30 August 1979 with the 15.00 Paddington-Swansea service, while Class 47 No 47500 *Great Western* heads towards London on the up relief line with an aggregate train bound for Acton Yard. *CJM*

Above: A view from the days before Trailer Guard Standard (TGS) vehicles were marshalled in HST sets to provide a comfortable working environment for the guard, now more usually known as a conductor. HST set No 253036 passes through the lush Cornish countryside at Cutmere, near Saltash, on 20 June 1980, forming the 10.10 Penzance-Paddington. *CJM*

Left: Passing the beautiful semaphore signal gantry at Taunton West on 28 March 1985, power car No 43125, leading the 07.25 Penzance-Paddington, slows for the station stop and a red signal at the London end of the station. Semaphore signals at this location and as far west as Paignton and Totnes were replaced by colour light signals as part of the West of England signal modernisation which saw a power signalbox opened at Exeter St Davids. *CJM*

Right: Marshalled in the original formation with two refreshment vehicles, set No 253025, with power cars Nos 43050/051 arrives at Swansea on 9 September 1977 with the 12.15 service from London Paddington. After only a short time in passenger service, the British Railways Board decided that just one refreshment vehicle would be formed in each set, reducing staff numbers and increasing the standard class seating as the vehicle was replaced by an additional TSO coach. *Les Bertram*

Above: Emerging from the western portal of Middle Hill Tunnel near Box on the London Paddington-Bristol main line, HST set No 253024, formed with power cars Nos 43048/049, operates the 13.45 Paddington–Weston-super-Mare service on 13 May 1980. Over the subsequent years many reallocations of power cars have taken place, and in 2005 these power cars were operated by Midland Mainline and allocated to Leeds Neville Hill depot. *CJM*

Above: In the days before East Coast electrification, when HSTs reigned supreme on InterCity London-Edinburgh and northern Scottish services, power car No 43154 passes Skelton Junction York on 9 September 1981 with the 13.00 Edinburgh-King's Cross service, in the period when two refreshment vehicles were formed in East Coast sets, marshalled back to back. *CJM*

Left: Formed with one refreshment vehicle, set No 254012 (formed with power cars Nos 43078/079) hurries past Biggleswade on 16 May 1980 forming an early morning Leeds-King's Cross service. *CJM*

Below: With Barford power station in the background, Class 254 set No 254004 (with power cars Nos 43062/063) heads north over the southern section of the East Coast main line on 16 May 1980 forming the 09.05 King's Cross-Leeds. *CJM*

Above: With the 'Edinburgh 200 miles' sign either side of the track, an immaculate HST set formed with power cars Nos 43093/057, taken in the days after the fixed formation trains and power car concept was abandoned, races south at Overton, north of York on 17 May 1982 with the 07.00 Edinburgh Waverley-King's Cross working. *CJM*

Below: HSTs first found their way onto traditional LM (London Midland) metals via Carlisle in 1979 when diversions were required due to the Penmanshiel tunnel collapse. The route from Newcastle to Scotland via Carlisle was a frequent diversionary route if the line between Newcastle and Edinburgh was blocked by engineering work or accident. On 26 April 1980, due to engineering work on the northern section of the ECML, set No 254028 departs Carlisle with the northbound 'Aberdonian' service. *G. S. Cutts*

Above: With the purpose-built Aberdeen Clayhills depot behind, the 10.25 Aberdeen-London King's Cross departs from the Granite City on 19 April 1982 led by power car No 43096. This power car has remained on the East Coast route and is now part of the GNER fleet. *Brian Morrison*

Below: On 11 September 1978, before full deployment of HST stock on the East Coast route, the 10.00 King's Cross-Edinburgh, the 'Flying Scotsman', passes East Linton in East Lothian on the approaches to the Scottish capital. The train is formed of twin refreshment car set No 254008, marshalled with power cars Nos 43071/070. *G. A. Watt*

Left: The Midland main line network from London St Pancras to Nottingham and Sheffield was the poor relation in terms of HST deployment, and it was not until 1983 that the fleet was introduced in any great numbers. On 28 June 1983, power car No 43102 passes Normanton-on-Soar forming the 11.35 Derby-London St Pancras. This power car was later named *HST Silver Jubilee* by the author of this book to mark the 25th anniversary of the HST fleet in the UK. *CJM*

Below: Passing beneath the Derby-Nottingham viaduct at Bennerley, the 16.00 Sheffield-London St Pancras, routed from Clay Cross (Chesterfield) to Loughborough via Nottingham, passes the site of Bennerley open-cast mine on 28 June 1983. The train is led by power car No 43067, a power car which later went to Virgin Trains and latterly operated by Great North Eastern Railway. *CJM*

Early Days: On the Midland Route

Above: The core formation for Midland Mainline HST sets was two first-class vehicles, one refreshment vehicle and four standard-class carriages, the first-class carriages being officially rostered for the London end of formations. On 27 June 1983, the 10.30 St Pancras-Sheffield passes Sutton Bonnington, traversing the northbound main line. *CJM*

Right: Sporting a 'Humber-Lincs Executive' stick-on headboard, used as part of an East Coast route introduction on the Hull line, power car No 43038, still sporting set No 253024, passes Normanton-on-Soar on 28 June 1983 forming the 10.35 Nottingham-St Pancras. The deployment of HST stock on the Midland main line route followed rationalisation and redeployment of sets used on the Western Region, hence this is a former Class 253. *CJM*

Left: With Ratcliffe Power Station, near Trent Junction, dominating the skyline, power car No 43111 leads the 12.30 Sheffield-London St Pancras service on 27 June 1983. This train is formed with the first class accommodation at the north end. *CJM*

Right: After departing from Derby and heading towards the Amber Valley, No 43188 approaches Duffield on 27 June 1983 with the 15.30 London St Pancras-Sheffield. On the 'up' line is a Class 120 DMU forming a Matlock-Derby working. *CJM*

Below Left: With a TGS marshalled as the first vehicle, the 09.25 Sheffield-London St Pancras passes Syston Junction on 18 May 1984 formed with power cars Nos 43085 and 43117. *CJM*

Below: Passing the site of the long closed Ilkeston station on 28 June 1983, power car No 43049 leads the 14.15 London St Pancras-Sheffield via Nottingham service. This power car later became the depot 'pet' at Leeds Neville Hill, carrying the depot's name on its side. *CJM*

Early Days: Cross-Country Routes

Above: Following authorisation for deployment of the HST fleet on the expanding, largely leisure-market CrossCountry routes, it was agreed to form these sets with just one first-class carriage to meet the extra standard-class patronage. On 29 June 1983, just a year after squadron CrossCountry introduction, power car No 43165 leads the 06.05 Bristol-Newcastle into Derby. *CJM*

Left: On 21 May 1982, just three weeks after the full HST deployment on CrossCountry operations, power car No 43178 leads the 06.03 Bristol Temple Meads-Newcastle past Dalton-on-Tees near Darlington. *CJM*

Above: With standard-class accommodation at the south end of the formation, the 06.20 Bradford-Paignton CrossCountry service departs from Derby on 29 June 1983 led by power car No 43188, which was later named *City of Plymouth* and is now in the First Great Western fleet. *CJM*

Right: One of the ongoing problems with the CrossCountry network was that passengers never knew at which end of the train first-class accommodation would be located. This was caused by the number of times that CrossCountry services changed direction during their journey. With first class at the south end, the 09.15 Edinburgh-Penzance approaches Darlington on 19 May 1982 led by power car No 43187. *CJM*

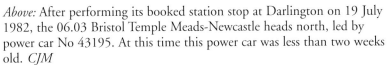

Above: After performing its booked station stop at Darlington on 19 July 1982, the 06.03 Bristol Temple Meads-Newcastle heads north, led by power car No 43195. At this time this power car was less than two weeks old. *CJM*

Above: With semaphore signalling and 'up' and 'down' loops still *in situ* at Exminster, south of Exeter, power car No 43185 heads west on 7 September 1982 with the 08.15 Birmingham New Street-Plymouth service. *CJM*

Left: Viewed just west of Totnes and climbing Rattery bank, power car No 43179 leads the 09.18 Edinburgh Waverley-Penzance service on 7 September 1982. This power car later became the flagship of Plymouth Laira depot, being named *Pride of Laira* on 15 September 1991, and is now part of the First Great Western fleet. *CJM*

Right: Traversing the down relief track between Filton Junction and Dr Days Junction (Bristol) on 8 June 1982 and passing close to the site of the closed Horfield station, the 12.37 Newcastle-Plymouth service is led by power car No 43187. The two relief tracks on the right of this picture were removed in the mid-1980s under route rationalisation, generating a 'bottleneck' for services between Bristol Temple Meads and Bristol Parkway. *CJM*

The InterCity Era

Above: The HSTs arguably looked their best in InterCity (IC) colours. This Western Region-allocated set No 253041, with power car No 43163 leading, passes Old Hill near Aldermaston on 8 July 1986 forming the 06.18 Penzance-London Paddington service. *CJM*

Left: Captured during the livery transition period between blue and grey and the first InterCity 'executive' colours, a southbound CrossCountry service passes Clay Cross Junction between Chesterfield and Derby on 18 September 1987. By this time the Class 253 and 254 set numbers on the front end were giving way to Class 43 power car numbers, shown here with a large 43040 applied below the front cab window. *CJM*

Above: The executive InterCity colours were more quickly applied to power cars than trailer passenger stock, meaning that for many months in the mid-1980s complete rakes of blue/grey-liveried passenger formations were 'top and tailed' by new liveried power cars. On 25 March 1987, No 43180 leads the 16.05 Paddington-Paignton via Bristol service out of Twerton Tunnel near Bath. *CJM*

Below: In full InterCity 'Executive' colours, the 08.33 Plymouth-York CrossCountry express departs from Birmingham and passes Washwood Heath on 2 March 1987, formed with power car No 43180 at the helm, which for some reason was carrying the numbers '5305' on the front end. *Chris Morrison*

Above: Sporting its Class 43 number on the front end, No 43120 leads the 11.45 Nottingham to London St Pancras service approaching Neilson's sidings, Wellingborough on 28 October 1987. Power car No 43097 brings up the rear of the train, which is formed with the first-class accommodation at the north end. *Dennis R. Wilkins*

Left: With the application of names, power cars painted in the first style of InterCity 'executive' colours received their cast nameplates on the section between the cab door and radiator compartment, centrally positioned below the InterCity125 brand name, rather than in more recent times when cast names have been applied between the luggage door and radiator compartment. On 11 March 1987 power car No 43113 *City of Newcastle upon Tyne* forms the rear vehicle of the 11.50 Nottingham-London St Pancras service departing from Leicester. *W. A. Sharman*

Above: With a full rake of blue and grey-liveried passenger stock, InterCity-liveried power car No 43129, carrying set No 253030, pulls onto the Plymouth line at Aller Junction, west of Newton Abbot on 17 April 1987 forming the 07.25 Paddington-Penzance service. This picture was taken in the period immediately prior to the introduction of colour light signalling in the West Country and the rationalisation of much infrastructure. Note the down goods loop line has recently been removed. *CJM*

Right: Route rationalisation was also the 'in' phrase in Cornwall in the 1980s when the route from Burngullow to Probus was singled, a section which was returned to double track in 2004 due to traffic growth. Taking the single line at Burngullow on 9 April 1990, No 43031 leads the 10.25 Paddington-Penzance service. *CJM*

Left: Looking very smart with all vehicles painted in the same livery, the 09.55 Penzance-Paddington passes Tremerton, near Saltash in Cornwall on 9 April 1990, led by power car No 43027 *Westminster Abbey*, a name which was applied on 29 May 1985 and removed in May 1990. The car was subsequently renamed *Glorious Devon* in April 1994. *CJM*

Below: On 4 November 1986, Western Region power car No 43142 was named *St Mary's Hospital Paddington* in a ceremony at Paddington station, when cast nameplates were unveiled by Sir Roger Bannister, the first four minute-mile runner and a graduate from the hospital. Carrying its set number 253036, the immaculate power car is seen two days after naming, passing West Drayton at the head of the 06.00 Plymouth-Paddington service. *CJM*

Right: At the time when British Rail was concentrating on the development of its established InterCity brand, the new InterCity colour scheme was formed, devised by staff from the InterCity sector and engineers from Derby. To demonstrate a train in the new colours, a full set was repainted and then used on Sunday 25 September 1983 for filming purposes around the scenic Copy Pit route. Carrying set No 253028, the train passes Hebden Bridge on its way to Copy Pit. *Gavin Morrison*

Below: Nearing Copy Pit summit, the filming train is about to be positioned for both movie and stills photography, which was subsequently used in a major advertising campaign for the InterCity brand. *John S. Whiteley*

Right: The British Rail InterCity 'Swallow' brand and livery was introduced in 1987, devised by design consultancy group Newell & Sorrell, and always looked very pleasing on the body design of the HST fleet. On 21 August 1992 power car No 43098 slowly departs from Glasgow Central for Polmadie depot with empty stock off the 07.52 Penzance-Glasgow working. On the left, Class 86/4 No 86415 awaits departure to London with the overnight Royal Mail service. *CJM*

Below: A small batch of power cars, Nos 43013/014/065/067/068/080/084/123, were adapted in 1987-88 by the Engineering Development Unit, Derby and Stratford Works to operate as surrogate Driving Van Trailers (DVTs) on the East Coast, due to late delivery of Mk4 driving cars. The modification work included provision of conventional buffers and draw hook, as well as a Time Division Multiplex (TDM) remote control system. After delivery of Mk4 DVTs the modified HSTs were absorbed into the core fleet. On 6 July 1993, No 43067 passes Clay Cross Junction leading the 06.48 Dundee-Penzance service. *CJM*

Below Right: Par station in Cornwall, where the branch line to/from Newquay connects with the main line system, is served by the HST network between London Paddington and Penzance. On 19 May 1995 power car No 43125 leads the 09.35 Paddington-Penzance into the Great Western-design station. *CJM*

Above: Pulling around the tight curve at the foot of Dainton bank at Aller Junction, a full InterCity 'Swallow'-liveried HST led by power car No 43194 forms the 08.40 Penzance-Paddington service on 6 June 1993. *CJM*

Below: Western Region-allocated HST sets commenced use on the Euston-North Wales Coast route in the 1990s, with stock operating empty from and to Old Oak Common. On 11 September 1993, power car No 43161 *Reading Evening Post* brings up the rear of the 09.06 Holyhead-London Euston at Chester. *Chris Dixon*

Right: Led by power car No 43127, the 16.20 Penzance-Paddington crosses Hayle Viaduct over Hayle Harbour and into Hayle station on 19 May 1995. The water inlet at this point goes into the main channel via St Ives Bay, behind the photographer. *CJM*

Below: The town of Southampton has two Freightliner-operated terminals, one located adjacent to Southampton Water and known as Southampton Maritime Terminal, and a smaller domestic terminal located at Millbrook, which on 17 July 1996 is passed by power car No 43098 leading the 06.17 Manchester Piccadilly to Bournemouth CrossCountry service. *Brian Morrison*

Above: After being made redundant on the East Coast route, following delivery of Mk4 DVTs, the buffer-fitted power cars were deployed on CrossCountry operations. On 22 April 1994, No 43123 leads the 12.20 Bournemouth-Newcastle service at Leamington Spa. *CJM*

Below: With a 1963-design 'slam-door' unit in the up siding at Southampton, power car No 43184 heads westward from the city on 3 July 1995 forming the 08.17 Manchester Piccadilly-Bournemouth service. *CJM*

Above: Following electrification of the East Coast route from London to Edinburgh and Glasgow, a number of HST sets were retained for use on Skipton, Hull, Aberdeen and Inverness services. Led by power car No 43120, the 10.30 King's Cross-Aberdeen pulls round the tight curve at Burntisland on 21 August 1992. *CJM*

Right: Shortly after the introduction of Eurostar International services from London Waterloo to Paris and Brussels, a small number of InterCity 'link' services ran to Waterloo to provide a connection. On 21 May 1996, the 10.46 Waterloo-Cardiff awaits departure, led by power car No 43151. *CJM*

Above: On a number of occasions HST sets have been used for charter or railtour services. One such trip was on 21 January 1989 when, led by power car No 43107, a set operated from London to Sheffield, Barnsley, Penistone, Leeds and Ilkley. It is shown here passing Apperley Junction, near Shipley. *Les Nixon*

Below: Skirting along the North Wales Coast route near Penmanmawr on 5 September 1997, the 09.50 Euston-Holyhead service, by this time operated by Virgin Trains West Coast, is formed of power cars No 43041/166, flanking seven trailer vehicles. *Russell Ayre*

Above: Apart from the CrossCountry Aberdeen-Penzance service, the longest HST operation was, and still is, the London King's Cross-Inverness route. On 31 March 1996, power car No 43114 leads the 09.40 departure from Inverness bound for London via Perth and Edinburgh. *CJM*

Right: With the closed Great Western signalbox of South Brent on the left side, then in use as a permanent way cabin, the 07.22 Penzance-Edinburgh CrossCountry service hurries past on 5 June 1995, led by power car No 43197. Brent was once the junction station for the Kingsbridge branch, which closed its doors to passengers in September 1963. *CJM*

Great Western Trains

Above: With the onset of UK railway privatisation in the mid-1990s came a mass of new train liveries and brandings. The first HSTs to emerge in company colours were for the Great Western franchise which took over the former Western Region operation. The company adopted a white and green colour scheme, with a Merlin logo on the body side. Perhaps with hindsight white was not an ideal colour to keep clean. The official livery launch train, with power car No 43193 nearest the camera, is viewed at Bristol Temple Meads on 30 September 1996. *CJM*

Below: Looking striking in its green and white colours, a full Great Western-liveried HST set, led by power car No 43139 passes along the banks of the River Teign at Shaldon Bridge on 22 February 1997 with the 08.08 Penzance-Paddington service. *CJM*

Above: The application of new liveries in the privatisation era has largely consisted of stick-on decals applied to a core background colour, thus livery changes have been relatively easy to make. Looking impressive against a dark stormy sky, a Great Western-liveried HST set led by power car No 43190 travels at 125mph through Shrivenham on 5 November 1997 forming a Paddington-Bristol Temple Meads service. *Russell Ayre*

Below: With Bruton parish church behind, an 'up' Great Western HST formation passes the Wiltshire town on 16 August 1997 with power car No 43188 in view. Bruton is located at the western end of the Berks & Hants line between Frome and Castle Cary and the majority of Great Western Paddington-Plymouth/Paignton/Penzance services pass the town nonstop, with Bruton only served by the local Bristol-Westbury-Weymouth line services. *Russell Ayre*

Above: At Bishton, east of Newport, Gwent, the 'up' slow or local line crosses from the 'down' side of the line formation to the 'up' by means of a single-track flyover. On 22 April 2003 a Great Western 'fag-packet'-liveried HST, led by power car No 43164, forms the 11.30 Swansea-Paddington 'Saint David' service beneath the flyover. Following the takeover of the Great Western franchise by FirstGroup, a major revision to the green and white livery was undertaken, until a corporate livery scheme was developed.
Russell Ayre

Left: Painted in green, white and gold First Great Western livery, the 10.46 Paddington-Paignton summer relief service passes through Torre station between Newton Abbot and Torquay on 23 September 2000, led by power car No 43140.
Russell Ayre

Above: With the residential part of Newport, Gwent, as a backdrop, the 09.00 Paddington-Swansea service crosses over the River Usk on 1 March 1995, led by power car No 43182. Traffic capacity in the Severn Tunnel-Cardiff area requires four tracks (two up and two down) to be retained. Generally freight traffic uses the slow lines, closest to the camera, and the passenger services operate over the fast or main lines. *CJM*

Below: Emerging from the 512yd-long Parsons Tunnel, and running along the Teignmouth Sea Wall, the 08.45 Paddington-Penzance heads west on 28 September 2002, led by power car No 43020 *John Grooms*. When the original Merlin Great Western livery was replaced by the First style, the livery was applied in a stick-on wrap. *CJM*

Aller Divergence, to the west of Newton Abbot, Devon, where the lines to Paignton and Plymouth diverge, has been a favourite location for photography for many years, with a farm bridge crossing the quadruple section of line. On 8 April 2002, First Great Western-liveried power car No 43186 *Sir Francis Drake* heads west with the 13.33 Paddington-Plymouth service, while Regional Railways Class 150 No 150221 takes the down Paignton line with the 14.54 Exmouth-Paignton service. Another Class 150/2 awaits the up Plymouth line signal with a Newquay-Exeter via Paignton service. *CJM*

Virgin Trains

Above: Without any doubt the most impressive livery for an HST to emerge from privatisation was Virgin Trains red, which looked quite stunning on the body profile of a High Speed Train set. The very first 'red set' to emerge from Leeds Neville Hill depot with power cars Nos 43063/068 was released on 3 January 1997 and worked via the Settle & Carlisle line to Edinburgh on 4 January for the official launch of Virgin Trains on 5 January. A special photostop was made during the journey north at Dent where the train is seen after a seasonal snowfall. *CJM*

Below: Taken during the extended period of livery transition from InterCity Swallow to Virgin red, power car No 43197 *Railway Magazine Centenary 1897-1997* heads south at Low Gill on 5 August 2000 with the 06.50 Edinburgh Waverley to Bournemouth. Repainting of the Virgin fleet took place at Leeds Neville Hill, Plymouth Laira depot and at Eastleigh Works. *Russell Ayre*

Above: With its first class seating end nearest the camera, the 09.25 Penzance-Edinburgh climbs Shap on 25 May 2003 with power car No 43122 *South Yorkshire Metropolitan County* in charge. When operating over the northern or mountain section of the West Coast route the superior power of the HST was demonstrated at its best. *Russell Ayre*

Below: On 4 April 1997, one of the only full Virgin-liveried HST sets in traffic at the time, led by No 43063 *Maiden Voyager*, the first power car to be repainted and used on the official Virgin Trains launch service, climbs towards Whiteball Tunnel on the Devon-Somerset border with the 09.22 Penzance-Edinburgh service. *CJM*

Left: It has always been very rare for HST sets to carry anything but stick-on headboards, due to the design of the vehicle front ends and the lack of a permanent tail lamp bracket on which to attach a headboard. However, to mark the final demise of HST stock operating with Virgin Trains on a timetabled basis, the 08.40 Euston-Holyhead and 13.41 return on 21 May 2004 carried a cast 'Irish Mail' headboard. The historic last Virgin Trains-operated HST set, led by power car No 43065, waits to depart from Holyhead on its return run to Euston. After this train arrived in London, Virgin Trains returned five sets of Mk3 HST passenger stock and 13 power cars to owner Porterbrook Leasing. It is not surprising to note that more than 18 months later Virgin Trains still hired in HST sets for the summer peak season in 2005 to cope with passenger demand on long-distance services to Newquay and in December 2005/January 2006 to work a daily Leeds — Plymouth—York diagram. *Brian Morrison*

Below: Stenson Junction between Derby and Burton-on-Trent has been a favourite location for photographers for many years, with not only Derby-Birmingham services being seen but those on the Derby-Crewe and Trent Junction-Burton freight line as well. Passing over the somewhat rationalised

Above: In common with many operators Virgin Trains was a keen supporter of naming its traction, be it HST power cars or locomotives. The practice of adorning trains with names was resurrected in modern traction terms in the mid-1970s and since, over 3,000 names have been applied. A number of different styles of name has been used. Left above we see a standard type cast nameplate *City of Newcastle upon Tyne*, attached to power car No 43180 at Newcastle after unveiling by the Mayor of Newcastle Cllr Belle Nixon on 13 May 1998. The name shown top right is one of a few 'stick-on' names *Blackpool Rock* tried early on in the Virgin franchise, but which were not greatly accepted. *Blackpool Rock* was applied to power car No 43100 in a ceremony at Blackpool on 25 May 1998. Both: *CJM*

Above: Climbing past Narroways Junction between Bristol Temple Meads and Bristol Parkway, the 13.00 Plymouth-Leeds service is formed with its standard class accommodation at the north end on 25 June 1998. Traction is provided by power cars Nos 43093 and 43067. The line diverging off to the photographers right is the route to Severn Beach. *Russell Ayre*

Above: One of the most impressive railway structures in the UK is that of the Forth Railway Bridge in Scotland, where the main line between Edinburgh and Dundee crosses the Firth of Forth. Running on time on 9 August 2001, power cars Nos 43081 and 43008 make their way off the Forth Bridge at North Queensferry and commence the last leg of their long journey north forming the 07.20 Plymouth-Aberdeen. *Russell Ayre*

Below: Led by power car No 43008, one of the original Western Region cars in the mid-70s, the 11.20 Glasgow Central-Penzance Virgin CrossCountry train passes Cartland between Carluke and Craigenhill Summit on 27 January 2001. On the rear of the train is power car No 43088. When operating in the Glasgow/Edinburgh area, the Virgin HST fleet was maintained by Edinburgh Craigentinny Depot. *Ian Lothian*

Above: One of the prime hubs of rail activity in South Yorkshire is Sheffield, where all of the Virgin Trains CrossCountry services operating on the Birmingham-York corridor stop, providing an interchange with the South Yorkshire local network as well as trans-Pennine services. On 28 August 2002, No 43094 and 43092 flank the coaching stock of the 06.20 Plymouth-Newcastle service as it departs from Sheffield and heads towards Rotherham, Doncaster and the East Coast route. On the left, in another platform is a Midland Mainline HST set on a London St Pancras service. *CJM*

Below: In the days before EWS lost the Royal Mail contract, rakes of Travelling Post Office vans are stabled just West of Bristol Temple Meads station as power cars Nos 43071/184 head west with the 07.05 Leeds-Plymouth service on 5 September 2001. *CJM*

Above: The Great North Eastern Railway (GNER), a part of Sea Containers Ltd, won the East Coast Franchise in the first round of UK rail privatisation and in 2005 was awarded the continuation of the franchise based on the high quality of the operation. The GNER HST fleet is now all finished in a distinctive dark blue and red livery, and internally has been refurbished to a very high standard. On 22 June 2001, Colton South Junction on the East Coast just south of York is the location for power cars Nos 43115/039 forming the 16.00 King's Cross-Aberdeen service. *Russell Ayre*

Left: Led by power car No 43096 *Stirling Castle*, the 12.00 King's Cross to Inverness 'Highland Chieftain' service approaches Aviemore on the Highland main line on 1 August 2005. *Chris Perkins*

Above: With power car No 43114 leading, a southbound service from northern Scotland to King's Cross slows for its Doncaster stop on 24 July 2003. With their top speed of 125mph, the IC125 and IC225 Class 91-powered services on the East Coast can operate happily alongside each other without problem. *Richard Tuplin*

Below: With heavy frost lying in the fields, the 09.55 Inverness to King's Cross service passes Lathallan, between Polmont and Bo'ness Junction in Fife on 2 January 2002, formed with power cars Nos 43038 and 43108. Some of the early GNER repaints carried white 'GNER' branding, but this later changed to the gold as seen today. *Ian Lothian*

Above: Passing Jamestown, between Inverkeithing and North Queensferry on the climb to the Forth Bridge, Nos 43120 and 43038 provide power for the 11.50 Aberdeen-King's Cross service on 25 October 1998. Since taking over East Coast services, GNER has operated two northbound and two southbound services each day between Aberdeen and London, with the journey taking around seven hours. *Ian Lothian*

Left: Running under clear semaphore signals between Perth and Dunblane, the delayed Inverness-King's Cross express passes Blackford led by power car No 43107 on 30 December 2003. The scuff mark on the front valance was caused earlier in the train's journey when it struck a motor vehicle on Forteviot Crossing near Perth, seriously delaying the train's progress. *Ian Lothian*

Above: To provide extra Summer Saturday accommodation Virgin Trains hired in various other operators' HST stock in both 2004 and 2005. In 2004, on the peak Saturdays, a GNER HST operated empty from Leeds to Plymouth before forming a stopping service to Newquay and then the 09.25 Newquay-Newcastle. Led by power car No 43114, the northbound train approaches Middle Way Crossing, Par, on the Newquay line on 29 May 2004. *Sam Felce*

Right: The hiring-in of HST sets has been essential to Virgin Trains to meet passenger demands. On 2 July 2005, GNER power cars Nos 43116 and 43120 pass Rockstone Bridge, Dawlish with the 10.32 Paignton-Newcastle. Both these power cars carry bodyside branding 'London 2012 Candidate City' as part of the bid for London to hold the 2012 Olympic Games. *CJM*

Above: Two distinct liveries have been applied to the Midland Mainline fleet of HSTs. Following privatisation, a green, tan and orange scheme was launched on 10 February 1997; this remained the 'house colours' until a new National Express Group-led identity of dark blue was launched on 5 March 2003. Showing some of each colour scheme, the 15.30 Sheffield-St Pancras passes Duffield, north of Derby, on 23 April 2004 led by power car No 43046, with a rake of new-liveried stock. *CJM*

Left: Displaying the tan, green and orange livery, complete with 'Bambi' logo, No 43058 departs from St Pancras as the rear power car of the 10.00 St Pancras-Nottingham service on 17 September 1997. The area in which this illustration was taken is now totally rebuilt as part of the new St Pancras International station in preparation for Eurostar services to mainland Europe commencing in 2007. *CJM*

Above: Power car No 43054 arrives at Sheffield station on 28 August 2002 with the 08.30 service from St Pancras. This train is not only operating the wrong way round with the first-class carriages at the north end, but has only one first-class FO vehicle, coupled behind the near power car. On the far left is a Virgin Trains HST forming a CrossCountry service. *CJM*

Below: Midland Mainline power cars received a number of modifications over the years, including new front lamp groups, with individual lens units for each light, as shown here on No 43044, a named vehicle, *Borough of Kettering*, which has its cast plate applied in the standard position in front of the luggage van door. The view was taken at Derby on 16 May 2002. *CJM*

Above/Below: The old and new order of London St Pancras. The magnificent trainshed building at St Pancras, the London terminal for Midland Mainline services, has been totally rebuilt in recent years to accommodate the new London terminal of the Eurostar operation. In the view above, the traditional St Pancras is seen with four Midland Mainline HSTs awaiting departure during the evening peak, while the view below shows a Midland Mainline HST 'borrowing' what will eventually be the London St Pancras terminus for the Kent CTRL services when St Pancras International is completed. No 43072 *Derby Etches Park* awaits departure on 20 April 2004 as the 16.20 service for Sheffield. Only the power car and first coach are still in original Midland Mainline livery. Both: *Brian Morrison*

Above: Although many people considered that the revised Midland Mainline livery would weather badly, the striking image of white and grey passenger saloons offset with a blue band and contrasting blue power cars looks very smart. On 5 March 2003, the livery launch demonstration train passes Clay Cross Junction south of Chesterfield led by power car No 43074. *Richard Tuplin*

Below: The launch of the new Midland Mainline blue livery, with grey and white coaching stock vehicles took place on 5 March 2003 in a special roll-out event at Derby, and the operation of a media train to Sheffield and return. The demonstration train with power car No 43166 leading, and featuring both exterior and interior refurbishment, is seen at Sheffield awaiting return to Derby. *CJM*

First Great Western

Above: Following FirstGroup's takeover of the Great Western franchise, the company corporate livery was soon applied. Initially this consisted of a white, blue and pink 'swirl' at the cab ends, the white later being replaced by blue. On 15 July 2002, No 43003 approaches South Brent powering the 08.33 Paddington-Plymouth service. *CJM*

Right: During the livery transition period between 'fag packet' and FirstGroup 'Barbie' colours, No 43029 hurries through South Brent on 15 July 2002 leading the 09.42 Penzance-Paddington service. *CJM*

Below: The official launch of the 'Barbie' FirstGroup livery was held at St Philips Marsh on 25 July 2001 when power car No 43029, (recently returned to traffic following a long period in store) was unveiled. For the ceremony the vehicle was renumbered to 43001 and a stylised FirstGroup *'f'* was applied to the front horn grille; this was removed before it entered passenger service and the vehicle returned to its proper number. *CJM*

Above: Although part of the core First Great Western network, the branch line between Newton Abbot and Paignton sees few trains, usually one per day on weekdays and around four on peak summer Saturdays. It is therefore unusual to capture passing HSTs on the branch. On 21 August 2004, No 43187 on the right leads the 11.33 Paddington-Paignton service, while on the right power car No 43151 brings up the rear of the 14.10 service in the opposite direction. *CJM*

Above: Traversing the single line between Burngullow and Probus at Grampound Road on 29 May 2004, a full First Great Western-liveried HST set is led by power car No 43037 *Pennydarren*, forming the 09.33 Paddington-Penzance service. This section of single line railway, which was always a major bottleneck for operators, has now been re-doubled. *Sam Felce*

Below: On 20 June 2005 No 43192 *City of Truro* heads west through classic Cornish countryside at Brea on the approach to Camborne, forming the 15.35 Paddington-Penzance. Behind the train is Carn Brea and the monument visible to the left commemorates the local Basset family. To the right of the train is the sleepy village of Brea. *Sam Felce*

Above: Between Newton Abbot and Plymouth just one principal main line station exists at Totnes, where loop tracks feed the platform facilities. These loops are frequently used to pass slower passenger or freight services. On 12 January 2005, power car No 43168 starts the climb towards Plymouth with the 11.05 Paddington-Plymouth service. Parked in the middle line at Totnes is Virgin Trains Class 57/3 No 57304 with a Virgin Voyager set performing driver training duties. *CJM*

Left: With the freight-only line to Crugwallins, Drinnick Mill and Parkandillack diverging on the right, power car No 43170 *Edward Paxman*, named after the founder of the Paxman engine company, passes Burngullow, west of St Austell, in Cornwall on 3 June 2005 leading the 09.04 Penzance-Paddington. *CJM*

Above: Many of the photographic locations on the Great Western main line are quickly being covered in lineside foliage, making photography difficult in some locations. One such place is Whiteball Tunnel, the boundary between Devon and Somerset, where trees have virtually taken over. On 25 May 2005, power cars Nos 43140 and 43195 climb towards Whiteball Tunnel with the 10.05 Penzance-Paddington. *CJM*

Right: At a passing speed close to 250mph, power cars Nos 43135 and 43027 approach the camera near Cholsey on 19 November 2004 forming the 13.15 Bristol Temple Meads-Paddington service, while on the down main the 13.45 Paddington-Swansea hurries west. *Chris Perkins*

Above: The allocation of the First Great Western HST fleet is divided between Bristol St Philips Marsh depot in Bristol and Laira Depot, Plymouth, with both depots keeping the stock in pristine condition. Gleaming in the sun at Bristol Temple Meads Station on 12 April 2005, power car No 43169 has just arrived with the 13.30 service from Paddington. *CJM*

Left: Led by power car No 43013, with No 43040 *Bristol St Philips Marsh* on the rear, the 17.30 Swansea-Paddington First Great Western service passes Undy, near Severn Tunnel Junction, on 29 May 2005. *Brian Morrison*

Right: With the driver using the high-pressure screen washer to improve his vision ahead, power car No 43179 *Pride of Laira* pulls away from Bristol Parkway station with the 11.55 Cardiff Central-Paddington service on 31 August 2004. Power car No 43037 is coupled at the rear of the formation, which is passing the now closed Royal Mail sorting office at Bristol Parkway, only opened in the 1990s and left derelict after EWS lost the 'Mail by Rail' contract in 2004. *Russell Ayre*

Below: With the Great Western main line between Exeter and Taunton blocked at Whiteball Tunnel due to engineering work, power cars Nos 43031 and 43181 re-start the diverted 07.26 Penzance-Paddington away from Exeter Central station on 30 December 2003. The train was diverted via Honiton and Yeovil before regaining its normal route at Castle Cary. *Russell Ayre*

Below: For the winter timetable of 2002, Virgin Trains introduced 12 2+5 HST formations to operate alongside the expanding Voyager fleet. At that time it was planned that eight sets would be rebuilt under the 'Project Challenger' title, retaining refurbished short HSTs for Paddington-Birmingham CrossCountry operations, a project which was abandoned. However the 2+5 sets operated for around 18 months and worked over most CrossCountry routes. On 5 April 2003, Class 43 Nos 43157 and 43167 power a 2+5 set past Colton South Junction, south of York, with the 08.25 Plymouth-Edinburgh service. *Richard Tuplin*

Above: A 2+5 formation with a difference. Due to the non-availability of a Virgin power car, Midland Mainline No 43089 was hired to Virgin Trains on 14 May 2003 to operate a Leeds-Penzance and Penzance-Preston service. Leading the 15.30 Penzance-Preston, the Midland Mainline car (with incomplete livery) crosses Cockwood Harbour, near Starcross. *CJM*

Below: On Saturday 27 December 2003 the last of the 'on lease' HSTs was used by Virgin. Virgin marked the event by carrying stick-on headboards. No 43092 is seen arriving at Par with set XC57 and classmate No 43160 on the rear with the 06.43 Dundee-Newquay service. The train arrived at the Cornish resort 41 minutes late at 18.53 and then formed the last scheduled Virgin HST working, the 19.30 Newquay-Plymouth. *Sam Felce*

Above: A major problem in running 2+5 HSTs was passenger overcrowding on peak summer weekends on the popular holiday routes, such as the Newquay-Newcastle, where in 2002 passengers on some weekends were left behind. On 28 September 2002 a 2+5 formation with power cars Nos 43180 and 43087 passes Holcombe on the Teignmouth Sea Wall section with the 09.30 Newquay-Newcastle service. *CJM*

Below: The original plan for the 2+5 'Challenger' sets was to operate them on the Paddington to Birmingham route, where capacity should not have been a problem. On 26 April 2003, a Manchester-Paddington service formed with power cars Nos 43068 and 43158 passes Morton Cutting near Didcot. *Ron Cover*

Above: Led by power car No 43155 *The Red Arrows*, a 2+5 formation passes Brock, a few miles north of Preston on the West Coast main line on 8 April 2003. The train is the Edinburgh-Plymouth service, which in 2003 was routed north out of Edinburgh to Carstairs to join the West Coast route. *Fred Kerr*

Below: With the cooling towers of Didcot power station in the background, a 2+5 set with power cars Nos 43086 and 43197 heads along the 'up' Great Western main line towards Reading on 8 April 2003 with a Manchester Piccadilly-Poole service. This train was routed from Manchester to Birmingham, Leamington, Oxford, Didcot and Reading, when it would change directions and travel via Basingstoke and Southampton. *Ron Cover*

The 'Rio' Project

Above: Project 'Rio', operated by Midland Mainline in conjunction with the Strategic Rail Authority to provide an alternative Manchester-London St Pancras service while West Coast modernisation was underway, officially started with the summer 2003 timetable and operated until the end of the summer 2004 timetable. On 24 July 2003, power car No 43074 makes ready to depart from Manchester Piccadilly with the 09.47 to London St Pancras, while Virgin Pendolino No 390022 awaits to depart for Euston. *CJM*

Left: Project 'Rio' saw a number of former Virgin Trains-operated Class 43s transfer to Midland Mainline, finding a short fill-in of work for these sets prior to going into store. No 43007, an original Western Region car subsequently used by Virgin, is seen painted in Midland Mainline livery at Manchester Piccadilly on 24 July 2003, posed next to Pendolino set No 390022. *CJM*

Above: The launch of the Manchester Piccadilly-St Pancras service was on 18 May 2003, with a small event on board the 12.49 service from Manchester. Formed with power cars Nos 43156 and 43070, the train passes Edale in the Hope Valley.
Richard Tuplin

Right: Displaying both first- and second-generation Midland Mainline colours, the 16.47 Manchester Piccadilly-London St Pancras HST, led by power car No 43050 with No 43072 on the rear, passes New Mills South Junction on 26 April 2004. The operation of the Project 'Rio' trains via the Hope Valley put considerable pressure on this route, which already saw high levels of freight and secondary passenger flows.
Brian Morrison

Above: Powering through Grindleford station in the Hope Valley on 27 April 2004, ex-Virgin operated power car No 43155 *City of Aberdeen* heads an otherwise all-new Midland Mainline-liveried HST formation working the 12.49 from Manchester Piccadilly to London St Pancras. *Brian Morrison*

Left: Near Edale on 27 April 2004, the 11.47 from Manchester Piccadilly to London St Pancras is headed through the Derbyshire countryside by power car No 43159 at the helm of a full Midland Mainline-liveried passenger rake. *Brian Morrison*

Right: A number of the HST sets used for the Project 'Rio' service retained their Virgin Trains red and dark grey livery but were shorn of the Virgin name. Led by power car No 43155 *City of Aberdeen*, the 10.47 Manchester Piccadilly-London St Pancras hurries towards Toton on 24 June 2003. *CJM*

The New Measurement Train

Above: The first visit of the yellow-liveried New Measurement Train (NMT) HST to the South West occurred on 20 June 2003. Forming the 07.19 Reading-Plymouth, with power cars Nos 43014 and 43067, it skirts the bank of the River Exe at Starcross. *Russell Ayre*

Below: The New Measurement Train usually operates to the West Country every other Friday, working over the Paddington-Plymouth route. On 8 April 2005, the train, led by power car No 43062 with No 43013 on the rear, passes Dawlish forming the 10.15 Plymouth-Paddington service. *CJM*

Above: Non-buffer-fitted No 43062 leads the New Measurement Train into Doncaster West Yard, adjacent to Doncaster station, on 19 April 2004. In the main, this train is driven by Serco drivers, using local route conductors as needed around the country. *Richard Tuplin*

Below: With buffer-fitted No 43013 on the rear, the New Measurement Train awaits clear signals at Doncaster on 27 October 2003 while *en route* from Derby to Edinburgh. The additional camera box on the front end is clearly visible in this view. *Richard Tuplin*

Above: The 2+5 New Measurement Train set, led by power car No 43013 with No 43014 bringing up the rear, passes Creech, near Taunton, on 17 January 2004, forming the Saturday-only 12.20 Swindon-Taunton test train. After arrival, the train returned to Swindon, departing from Taunton at 14.46. *Brian Garrett*

Below: HSTs meet at Taunton on 20 September 2003; on the left a 2+5 Virgin Trains formation slows for a station stop with a northbound service, while the New Measurement Train departs from the down main platform into Taunton yard to facilitate a direction move before returning north. *Brian Garrett*

Above: Each of the principal main-line routes on the Great Western, Midland Mainline, Virgin West Coast and GNER networks are covered by the New Measurement Train at least once a fortnight. Some routes, such as the West Coast, are traversed weekly. On 17 March 2003 the train passes Oakley, north of Bedford, forming the 08.00 Derby Etches Park to Derby Etches Park via St Pancras and Bedford testing special. Motive power is provided by Nos 43062 and 43013. *Nigel Gibbs*

Right: The intermediate vehicles formed in the New Measurement Train are all of the Mk3 design, with the exception of car No 999550 which was a purpose built Mk2 test car. All vehicles in the train were rebuilt for NMT use, with the Mk3 trailers rebuilt from the frames upwards at Hunslet Barclay, Kilmarnock. Car No 977984 was rebuilt from Mk3 HST-designed TRUK No 40501. The coach now has staff mess facilities and a generator in the near end. The vehicle is seen at Doncaster. *Richard Tuplin*

Unusual Duties

Right: At various times during its 30 plus years in service, the HST fleet has operated or taken part in special events. In immaculate condition, sequential power cars Nos 43175/176 were used for three days of filming on the Todmorden-Burnley line on 9-11 December 1981. The filming special is seen near Portsmouth (Yorkshire) on 11 December 1981 after a slight covering of snow. *G. Roose*

Left: The InterCity operation based on the former Western Region, operating services from London Paddington to Swansea, Bristol, Plymouth and Penzance, relaunched the London-Bristol route on 4 October 1993 under the InterCity 'Shuttle' banner, offering at the time a 'turn up and go' service throughout the day, with a train always available for immediate boarding in both London and Bristol throughout the day. On the first day of operation a special press run was organised from Bristol to Paddington using pristine power car No 43126. In the days prior to overhead power lines being erected at Paddington the train arrived in the capital to be joined by a miniature InterCity 'Shuttle' hot air balloon. *CJM*

Above: On 8 August 1977, the first recorded use of an HST on the Royal Train took place when Western Region set No 253025 was reformed with three FOs and a refreshment vehicle and conveyed Her Majesty the Queen from London to the South West. Returning empty stock to Bath to collect the Royal party, the train is seen passing Bathampton Junction. *Philip Fowler*

Right: Over the years a number of HSTs have been requested to operate charter services, frequently taking the class to pastures new. One such event was on 18 March 1990 when Hertfordshire Rail Tours operated a set to Barnstaple in North Devon, seeing the first visit of a class member to the 'Tarka Line'. Led by power car No 43099, the train approaches Copplestone. *CJM*

Above: One of the most unusual workings with an HST in Devon was on 10 December 2000 when power cars Nos 43182/019 were coupled back-to-back and used as a locomotive to haul a defective HST set, with power cars Nos 43042/024, from Exeter to Plymouth, seen passing Dawlish. *CJM*

Left: Following accident damage First Great Western TSO No 42361 was repaired and used as a mobile office and development coach at Bristol St Philips Marsh Depot, where it was mounted on a short section of track and renumbered to 42000. It is pictured on 21 August 2003. Due to stock shortages the vehicle was later returned to passenger traffic. *CJM*

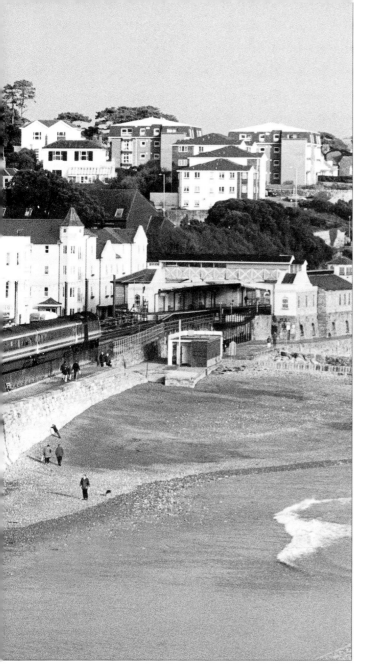

Top/Middle/Above/Left: A large number of naming ceremonies have been held over the years involving HST power cars. A small selection is shown here. Sir Richard Branson (top) named No 43093 *Lady in Red* at Manchester on 2 February 1997. The Mayor of Penzance, Primrose May, unveiled the name *Golowan Festival Penzance* on power car No 43078 at Penzance on 22 June 1996. *The Railway Heritage Trust* name was unveiled on car No 43189 by Sir Peter Parker, Sir Bill McAlpine and Brian Scott, Managing Director of Great Western, on 10 October 1995. *The Irish Mail* stick-on name was launched at Euston on the side of power car No 43101 on 31 July 1998 by pouring Guinness over the name before the train set off to Holyhead. All: *CJM*

Above: At various times HST sets have operated off the UK national rail network and visited light or private railways. One such trip was on 4 April 1998 when a Pathfinder Tour visited Kingswear on the Paignton & Dartmouth Railway. Formed of a Great Western passenger rake and power cars Nos 43022 and 43146, the train travels through Churston station and past the part-restored Class 50 No 50002. *CJM*

Below: Following the replacement of all Virgin Trains-operated HSTs with Voyager stock, a number of sets were stored at different locations. Several redundant sets were purchased by FirstGroup, with some vehicles stored on the West Somerset Railway at Minehead. Power cars Nos 43094/123 flank a five-car formation in Minehead sidings on 16 April 2005. *CJM*

Above: After Midland Mainline's Project 'Rio' services ended in September 2004, several of the off-lease HSTs were transferred to First Great Western. A major stock move took place on 12 September 2004 when Freightliner Heavy Haul was contracted to haul three HSTs from Manchester Longsight to Plymouth Laira. Midland Mainline-liveried Class 43s Nos 43180/088 and a passenger rake are hauled past Cockwood Harbour, Devon by Class 47 No 47150. *CJM*

Left: On 13 September 2004, four of the former Midland Mainline power cars, Nos 43156/195 and 43079/063, were hauled from Plymouth Laira to Bristol St Philip Marsh by Freightliner Type 4 No 47805 for repainting into First Great Western colours and fitting of Automatic Train Protection equipment. The stock move is seen passing Dawlish Warren. *CJM*

Right: High-speed trains of two different generations meet at Polmadie Depot, Scotland on 5 June 1997. On the left is Virgin Trains power car No 43155 which has just arrived for overnight cleaning after forming a Penzance-Glasgow working. On the right is North of London Eurostar set No 373308 which at the time was stabled at Polmadie Depot while involved in type test approval of Eurostar stock in the Glasgow area in preparation for the then proposed introduction of a Glasgow-Paris Eurostar service. *CJM*

Above: Short-formed HSTs have operated on a number of occasions for a variety of reasons. Here a three-car HST, formed with two refreshment vehicles and a TGS with the power cars from East Coast set No 254035, passes Wellingborough on the Midland main line on 20 August 1982 during a period of driver training. *Michael Ricks*

Left: Another view of the same short formation is seen at Loughborough on 27 August 1982 when the set was being used on a Cricklewood-Derby training run. Training using short-formed sets was fine for driver familiarisation, but the braking technique for such a short train was considerably different from handling a full-length 2+8 formation. *I. J Hodson*

Above: Short-length HST sets have sometimes operated for traction testing purposes, such as this case on 28 June 1983 when a specially formed set was used over the Preston-Carlisle section of the West Coast route at speeds up to 125mph. Led with a power car from set No 253043, the five-vehicle set approaches Carlisle. *Colin Keay*

Below: As part of the driver training programme for West of England crews on HSTs, a short 2+2 rake was formed up in 1979. Led by a power car from set No 253017, the GTi HST formation passes Totnes on 26 July bound for Newton Abbot from Plymouth. *Roger Penny*

Left: The movement of single HST power cars around the network has always been frowned upon, mainly for the reason of lack of conventional couplings if the vehicle should fail. For that reason a batch of barrier vans was converted, largely from ex-passenger stock, to 'escort' light power car moves. On 30 October 1980 a Class 254 power car with a Mk2 barrier passes the closed Carcroft and Adwick-le-Street station while travelling 'light' from Neville Hill Depot to Bounds Green Depot. *CJM*

Right: The running of short HSTs, actually conforming to light locomotive running is quite common practice for transferring power cars between depots. However, on occasions special events have required power car movements. On 25 June 2005 a very special event in railway circles took place at Exeter St Davids, when First Great Western power car No 43139 was named *Driver Stan Martin 25 June 1950 - 6 November 2004.* Stan Martin was the driver at the controls of power car No 43019 leading the 17.35 Paddington-Plymouth, which collided with a road vehicle at Ufton Nervet level crossing on 6 November 2004. Sadly Stan was killed and FirstGroup in his memory named a power car as a lasting tribute. The cast nameplates were unveiled by his widow Deborah. With MTU-fitted power car No 43009 for company, No 43139 is seen in platform 2 at Exeter St Davids just prior to naming. *CJM*

Left: With the Western Region and latterly First Great Western having two principal maintenance depots, one located in Plymouth and the other in Bristol, frequent power car and stock transfer moves are needed to balance operations. On 2 November 1988 InterCity125-branded power car No 43174 pulls off the Plymouth line at Aller junction, Newton Abbot with a Plymouth Laira to Bristol St Philips Marsh move. A Mk1 HST barrier coach is coupled on the rear. *CJM*

Right: To mark the 125th anniversary of Paddington station, a number of events were carried out on 1 March 1979. This included a run on the main line of preserved Great Western 'King' No 6000 *King George V* and a display of rolling stock old and new at Paddington station. One of the exhibits was new HST power car No 43048 and a TS passenger carriage, together with Great Western 'Hall' No 5900 *Hinderton Hall*. *Brian Stephenson*

Below: Following attention at Bristol St Philips Marsh, a transfer move to Laira depot on 29 August 2004 led to this 2+2 HST being operated. Formed of power cars Nos 43125 and 43010, the train consisted of buffet car No 40208 and TS No 42076. The GTi HST is seen awaiting the signal to clear at Aller Junction, Newton Abbot. *CJM*

A Helping Hand

Above: On numerous occasions HST sets have required assistance by locomotives, either due to failures in service or transfer between depots. On 1 May 1984, the 08.10 Newcastle-Plymouth, formed with power cars Nos 43036/037, failed *en route* and was assisted forward from Exeter by 'Peak' No 46028. The train is seen near Matford, Exeter. *Peter Medley*

Below: On 6 May 1993, power car No 43191 was hauled by Class 37 No 37098 from Bristol St Philips Marsh depot to Plymouth Laira following failure of the engine turbocharger, identified by the covering of the bodyside with oil. The transfer move is seen crossing Cockwood Harbour, while Type 3 No 37671 approaches with a St Blazey-Exeter freight. *CJM*

Above: On 3 September 2004, Porterbrook 'spot-hire' HST set Nos 43092/122 were hired to Virgin Trains to work on the Birmingham-Manchester route. While forming the 10.51 Birmingham New Street-Manchester, it failed near Wolverhampton and was taken to Oxley Depot by Type 4 No 47830. Later in the day, the set was hauled to Leeds Neville Hill Depot by DRS Class 37/0 No 37229 as the 14.30 Oxley-Neville Hill, seen passing Portobello Junction. *Glen Flurry*

Below: One of the more interesting HST 'drags' took place on 21 July 2002, when First Great Western Class 47 No 47830 was used to haul power car No 43005 and TS No 42076 in First 'fag packet' green livery, two barrier vans and a complete HST passenger rake in FirstGroup corporate livery from Bristol St Philips Marsh Depot to Laira Depot. The combination is seen passing Cockwood Harbour, Devon. *CJM*

Left: Due to the failure of GNER power cars Nos 43039 and 43115 on 29 April 2004, just prior to departure of the 15.30 King's Cross to Edinburgh service, the train was piloted throughout by Class 91 No 91132. The unusual formation of an electric locomotive piloting an HST is seen passing Fenwick between Doncaster and York. *Richard Tuplin*

Below: On the final 'peak' Saturday of the 2004 season, 4 September, Virgin Trains 06.35 Manchester-Newquay, formed with power cars Nos 43098/153, failed *en route* to the West with coolant faults. The return train, the 14.20 Newquay-Manchester, was piloted from Plymouth by EWS Class 37/4 No 37425 that ran light from Newport to work the train. With many haulage enthusiasts obviously on board, the historic train, which should have been the last-ever Virgin Trains-liveried HST from Cornwall and Devon, passes Aller, west of Newton Abbot. *CJM*

Above: With a reducing number of Virgin Trains HSTs following the introduction of Voyager sets, a number of HSTs were transferred to Manchester Longsight for use by Midland Mainline on its Project 'Rio' services. On 29 March 2002, Freightliner Heavy Haul was contracted to haul a complete HST set with power cars Nos 43157 and 43090 from Plymouth Laira to Derby Etches Park with Type 4 No 47289. The train passes along the famous Dawlish Sea Wall, while sea defence work was ongoing following winter storms. *CJM*

Below: Disaster struck Virgin Trains on the first summer Saturday of the 2005 season, 28 May, when a hired-in Porterbrook 'spot-hire' HST, formed with power cars Nos 43070/080 and an ex-Midland Mainline 'Rio' passenger set, failed at Lostwithiel while forming the 15.22 Newquay-Manchester. After passengers were detrained, First Great Western provided Class 57/6 No 57604 *Pendennis Castle* to haul the defective set to Laira Depot for attention. The convoy of a First Great Western Class 57, a GNER-liveried power car and a 'Rio' passenger set passes Devonport Dockyard station in the last rays of evening light. *Sam Felce*

Mishaps

Above: The most serious accident to involve an HST came at 18.11 on 6 November 2004, when the 17.35 Paddington-Plymouth, formed of vehicles 43019, 44006, 42020/017/022/018, 40206, 41014/013 and 43029, collided at around 100mph with a motor car parked on Ufton Nervet level crossing, between Theale and Aldermaston on the Berks & Hants main line. In normal circumstances, if trains hit motor vehicles on crossings, even at high speed, the road vehicle is propelled out of the train's path. However, on this occasion the results led to a catastrophic derailment of all vehicles of the train and the deaths of seven people: five train passengers, the train's driver and the driver of the road vehicle. The leading wheel of the train derailed, and struck a facing point blade just a few yards ahead which led to the accident. This was the view three days after when recovery of the vehicles was about to commence. *Alan Smith*

Above: The rear power car involved in the Ufton Nervet collision on 6 November 2004, No 43029, which although damaged, was not destroyed and indeed, after being the subject of a huge enquiry and investigation followed by a period in store at Bombardier Crewe, has been returned to First Great Western for repair. This was the angle at which No 43029 landed after its deceleration from 100mph to zero in little more than the train's length. The points which steered the leading power car into derailment are seen in the foreground. *Alan Smith*

Below: Another power car which was all but destroyed in a high speed collision was No 43173, which was leading the 10.32 Swansea-Paddington service on 19 September 1997 when, after passing a signal at danger, it collided at high speed with a freight train at Southall. The impact cut one side off the power car allowing this extraordinary picture to be taken during the recovery operations on 22 September. *Roland Kennington*

Left: Over the years Newton Abbot in Devon has proved not to be the safest location for HST travel, with two HST accidents. On 25 March 1994, the 07.20 Penzance-Glasgow was waiting time in the station when the rear power car, No 43071, was struck by Class 158 No 158833 forming the 09.40 Paignton-Cardiff. This was the resultant damage at just 10mph. *CJM*

Left, Above and Right: A far more serious accident occurred at Newton Abbot on 7 March 1997 when, due to an axle journal failure, the 15.35 Paddington-Penzance became totally derailed, with one vehicle left straddling a river bridge. The train was powered by Nos 43130/170 which were not damaged. On the left, vehicle No 42078 sits atop the river bridge, while above, power car No 43170 awaits rerailing of its inner bogie. On the right the train's buffet car No 40710, which ended up at almost 45deg onto its side, is lifted by road cranes and reunited with its wheelsets. All: *CJM*

Left: With the introduction of the HST fleet came a large investment in depot facilities, which in most cases had to be totally rebuilt to deal with the HST configuration, allowing simultaneous refuelling and servicing of power cars at either end of a fixed train consist. At Penzance new washing facilities were built, together with the rebuilding of the shed to deal with longer fixed formation trains. On 3 July 1982, set No 253004 passes through the Long Rock washing plant after arriving with a service from London.
Brian Morrison

Below: Plymouth Laira depot was considerably rebuilt for its HST role, with six new full-train-length carriage-servicing roads, together with significant alterations to depot servicing facilities, which in many areas had to be upgraded from dealing with diesel-hydraulic traction to state-of-the-art diesel-electric locomotives. Usually it is rare to find the carriage sidings full of stock during daylight hours, but on 3 February 1982 an ASLEF manning dispute saw many trains cancelled and the sidings full.
Roger Penny

Above: One of the principal depots on the East Coast main line dealing with HST operations following their introduction on the King's Cross route was Bounds Green in north London, where new purpose-built accommodation was provided. Power car No 43071 is seen supported on synchronised lifting jacks on 24 February 1987 while undergoing a traction motor change. *CJM*

Right: Although the HST fleet was constructed at BREL Crewe Works, the factory at Derby was charged with its overhaul needs for the first 15 years of service. On 30 September 1985, power car No 43055 receives a heavy overhaul in the main erecting shop at the Derby complex. *CJM*

Left: For many years the West of England maintenance facility at Plymouth Laira undertook repairs and service exams to Great Western and CrossCountry HST fleets, with capacity in the three- and later four-track HST shed being at a premium during the evening and night period. On 19 January 1996 CrossCountry power car No 43154 takes centre stage in the HST shed. Fuelling and power car-servicing equipment is positioned at the ends of the building and carriage servicing equipment is in the middle. *CJM*

Right: As mentioned previously, very few serious accidents have befallen the HST fleet in more than 25 years of operation. An incident which had serious ramifications took place just outside Edinburgh on 13 August 1994 when a runaway Class 37 collided with a northbound passenger train led by power car No 43180. The entire front end was ripped off in the accident and the train's driver had to be rescued. After spending some months at Edinburgh Craigentinny Depot, No 43180 was taken to BREL Crewe Works where this view was taken and repairs effected. No 43180 is now operating as part of the core First Great Western fleet. *CJM*

Left: In the closing years of Virgin Trains' HST operations, the general run-down condition of the fleet, with a long gap between major overhauls, was starting to show, with many power cars receiving attention at both Leeds Neville Hill and Plymouth Laira Depots. On 6 February 2001, No 43197 is seen inside the heavy repair lines at Laira depot for attention and the refitting of *The Railway Magazine* nameplates, which were carried until 18 August 2003. *CJM*

Right: As part of a desire to improve performance and reliability BR contracted Mirrlees Blackstone to supply four new MB190 power units in November 1985. The first power car to receive a new engine was No 43091, with the work undertaken at BREL Derby Works as part of the vehicle's classified overhaul. The work to install revised power units was extensive, with new floor brackets and bed plate required. The unit is shown here lifted for a trial installation on 18 August 1986. *BR*

Left: Under original maintenance contracts the HST passenger fleets were maintained by regional depots and received heavy overhauls at BREL Derby Litchurch Lane Works, the same facility that built the stock. In more recent years a number of other major works have undertaken HST overhauls, with the majority of work now undertaken by local depots. Western Region-allocated TRFB No 40734 is seen inside Derby Litchurch Lane on 11 March 1993 during refurbishment. On the left is a London Underground Metropolitan Line train part-way through refurbishment. *CJM*

Above: Under the privatisation banner, a number of facilities not previously associated with HST repairs were contracted to perform heavy general overhauls. One was Bombardier Doncaster, the former BREL site, which in recent years undertook work on GNER-allocated power cars. On 13 March 2001, No 43112 is seen on support stands while receiving a refurbishment overhaul. *CJM*

Left: The Wabtec site at Doncaster has also effected a number of HST repairs, modifications and engine changes in recent years. As the present facility does not have a suitable depot-mounted crane for power unit exchanges, these have to be done using a road crane outside the north end of the main erecting shop, as demonstrated here on 20 September 2004 with a power unit exchange on car No 43009, which failed while under test. *Derek T. Porter*

HST Passenger Vehicles

Above: The prototype HST train set incorporated two refreshment vehicles, a TRSB (Trailer Restaurant Standard Buffet) and a TRUK (Trailer Restaurant Unclassified Kitchen). The TRUK No 40500, the original 10100, is seen at Bath in March 1976. This vehicle later went to BR Research as Lab 21 (RDB977089) and is not part of the New Measurement Train. *John Glover*

Above: The same bodyshell was used in all production FO (First Open) and TS cars, allowing easy internal rebuilds if required. The same structural design speeded up construction and eased the need for spare parts. Internally, however, the vehicles are very different, even more apparent in the days of privatisation. InterCity-liveried FO No 41116 is shown. *CJM*

Right: It is amazing what just a different livery can do for the look of a passenger vehicle. Here FO No 41056 shows off the original Great Western Trains livery of ivory, white and green at Bristol Temple Meads. This vehicle shows the 1990s-applied central door-locking system, with the release light between the door and toilet window and the emergency release valve to the right of the number. *CJM*

Left: Sporting the first version of Midland Mainline livery, TSO (Trailer Standard Open) No 42225 is illustrated at Leicester. The toilet compartment windows were originally intended to house a roller route blind operated from inside the coach, but after a few trials on the original Western Region sets this was removed. Various attempts over the years have been given to installing route displays in this window, but none to date have been successful. *CJM*

Above: In 1993 a number of moves were made to refurbish the HST passenger environment. One was this re-fit of the standard class interior using 2+2 high-back seats in a mix of airline and group layouts. Note the mid-vehicle-length luggage stacks. *CJM*

Above: Following privatisation, Midland Mainline carried out a mini-refurbishment of vehicle interiors, retaining the original seat layout but using new trim. Mid-vehicle-length luggage stacks were installed. *CJM*

Above: The early-1990s first-class trial refurbishment saw the traditional 2+1 seating style retained, but mid-vehicle-length glass dividers were fitted at the time to separate smoking from non-smoking accommodation. Note the revised moquette. *CJM*

Above: In October 1994, InterCity in conjunction with ABB carried out a trial refurbishment of buffet car No 40754 at Derby Works. The first class seating area is shown, with new moquette, curtains and wall coverings. Sadly the project was not furthered. *CJM*

Above: A fleet of Mk3 Trailer Guard Standard (TGS) vehicles were built subsequent to the main HST building programme, following a policy to move the guard or conductor from the power car to a 'within train' position. The TGS fleet numbered in the 44xxx series has normal passenger doors at one end only, with a guard's office, luggage van and dedicated doors at the other. TGS vehicles are marshalled at the standard class end of the train, with the conductor's office adjacent to the power car. Midland Mainline No 44012 is illustrated. *CJM*

Above: In 1993 two InterCity business sector Market Test Vehicles were modified at the Engineering Development Unit, Derby to show what might be done to the HST passenger fleet. TGS No 44084 was totally rebuilt with an open-plan office, allowing the vehicle to be placed in the middle of formations. Together with a modified FO, the two vehicles operated on a number of routes in the immediate pre-privatisation period. *CJM*

Below: The original style and layout for the HST First Open (FO) vehicle, showing the 2+1 seating layout, tables by each seat and aluminium grab handles on seat backs. At this time, the moquette was finished in orange. *BR*

Above/Left: There has been much speculation as to what will happen in the long term to the HST fleet, which is without doubt the most successful diesel-powered passenger train design in the world. In 2004 FirstGroup, in association with Angel Trains, MTU and Brush Traction, set about a 'trial' re-engining of two Class 43s, Nos 43004/009. These have been fitted with a MTU 16V 4000 power unit, which is cleaner in emissions and uses less fuel than the existing Paxman engine. In the view above, No 43009 is seen carrying a short-lived Angel Trains all-over blue-livery at the Brush Works in Loughborough on 11 May 2005. On the left, power car No 43004 can be seen receiving final technical adjustments inside the main erecting shop at Brush Traction. Following the re-award of the Greater Western Franchise to FirstGroup, a squadron re-engining project commenced in January 2006 . Both: *UpMain*

Above: Although the MTU power unit had been bench-tested at Brush Traction, no active running trials of the design had been undertaken in the UK. As soon as the first power car was delivered to FirstGroup at Bristol, a static test programme commenced followed by some 'light' running in. Showing off its revised front lamp clusters, No 43009 is seen passing Langstone Rock, Dawlish Warren marshalled with TGS No 44059 and Paxman power car No 43027 on 26 May 2005 making its first run on the main line when it formed the 09.38 Bristol St Philips Marsh-Plymouth test special. Further 'light' and 'loaded' test runs operated and within two weeks certification was granted to allow the car into normal service. By mid-June the second of the rebuilt cars was in daily traffic. *CJM*

Above: Could this be the way forward for the HST? This is the stunning exterior design of a prototype HST2 or 'Venturio' project put forward to the UK rail industry and especially the lease companies by Siemens Transportation. The conceptual train, which owes much of its design to the German ICE family, could have end power cars and distributed train power or, if preferred, underfloor power plants. *CJM*

Left: With the majority of HST power cars not having conventional draw gear, each vehicle carries an emergency adaptor coupler which, after opening the centre section of the front valance, can be attached to an eye. This metal tube then has a slot head connector attached to the end which, if required, can be attached to any locomotive with a conventional coupling hook. Air connections are also provided, allowing a locomotive's main reservoir and brake pipe to be connected, permitting an HST train to be assisted by a normal locomotive (diesel or electric) if needed. The same front-end valance also protects a train supply connection, allowing HST stock to be 'pre-heated' with the engine shut down; this is ideal for depots where exhaust contamination could be dangerous, or at busy stations. *CJM*

Right: The HST power car bogie design is classified as BP16: cars Nos 43002-123/153-198 are fitted with Brush traction motors, with the balance using GEC traction equipment. The inner end bogie of power car No 43104 is illustrated following a heavy general overhaul. *CJM*

Below: Driving cab layout of First Great Western power car No 43009. This vehicle is fitted with Automatic Train Protection (ATP) equipment, located to the right of the cab central section. The fitting of ATP saw some equipment repositioned. This example has driver's reminder appliance, modified windscreen-wiper controls and hazard warning lights. *CJM*

Above: Emerging from the eastern portal of Dainton Tunnel, located between Totnes and Newton Abbot on the Great Western main line to the West Country, original-liveried power car No 43133 leads the 08.27 Penzance-Paddington service on 6 July 1984. This power car was delivered to BR Western Region in July 1979 and has remained working over the same route all its life. *CJM*

Below: A view that cannot be repeated today, showing Old Oak Common from the Mitre Bridge line. On the left is Old Oak Common signalbox, while in the foreground on the left the (now closed) line to North Pole Junction diverges. On 31 October 1978 HST set No 235014 approaches London on the 'up' main, while another HST set enters Old Oak Common carriage sidings. *CJM*

Above: Taking the down main line at Exminster, an HST set led by power car No 43148 forms the 08.05 Paddington-Plymouth service on 7 September 1983. On the left the Exminster by-pass 'Sannerville Way' is seen under construction, while the new M5 motorway is seen in the background. *CJM*

Below: In the days before Trailer Guard Standard (Second) vehicles were inserted into sets, the 11.15 Paddington-Bristol Temple Meads approaches Sonning Cutting between Twyford and Reading on 4 March 1980, led by power car No 43120, a vehicle delivered in 1977 as a 'spare' and thus without a set number on the front. *CJM*

Right: With the clay dryer chimneys at Par Harbour in the background, Western Region domestic HST set No 253020 awaits departure from Par station on 7 June 1980 with the 09.42 Penzance-Paddington service. In the background is Par station yard, housing a short Mk1 passenger rake off a morning Plymouth-Par stopping service. A quarter of a century later and the basic layout remains largely unchanged, Par still using semaphore signals. *CJM*

Below: Led by power car No 43016, the 09.25 Plymouth-Paddington service passes Rewe between Exeter St Davids and Tiverton Parkway on 3 July 1984. This power car was delivered to the Western Region on 5 June 1976 and has remained a Western Region, Great Western Trains and First Great Western vehicle ever since. *CJM*

Above: Wearing the first of the InterCity 'executive' liveries, power car No 43173 leads a similarly-liveried set past Hungerford Common on the Berks & Hants line on 23 June 1989 forming the 14.10 Paddington-Penzance service. Sadly this power car was all but destroyed in the Southall collision on 19 September 1997 when it was the leading car of the 10.32 Swansea-Paddington express and struck a freight train crossing its path. *CJM*

Left: Carrying the yellow and black InterCity colours, power car No 43164 passes Weston Beacon near Ivybridge, Devon, on 17 April 1987, while forming the 14.05 Plymouth-Paddington service. This vehicle, like many others at the time, retained its 253-prefixed set numbers on the nose end, even after repainting into InterCity or Executive colours. *CJM*

Above: The number of livery transition periods seen over the years has caused many 'mixed-livery' sets to be in operation, generating some extra interest for photographers. InterCity-liveried power car Nos 43025 and 43181 approach Taunton on 28 March 1985 forming the 08.33 Plymouth-York CrossCountry service. *CJM*

Below: Showing the full InterCity 'Swallow' livery, a scheme which suited the HST bodylines well, power car No 43169 leads the 06.40 Penzance-Paddington past Berkley on 31 May 1996. *CJM*

One of the most picturesque locations in the UK at which to photograph trains is the South Devon Sea Wall, located between Dawlish Warren and Teignmouth, giving good photographic views of trains spreading most of the way from Exeter to Newton Abbot, along the banks of the River Exe, past Lyme Bay and along the River Teign. With Dawlish in the background, power car No 43103 leads the 08.15 Leeds-Paignton service past Horse Cove on 23 June 1994. *CJM*

Above: The InterCity CrossCountry operation led to HST stock operating over the Southern Region third-rail territory from the 1990s, with a need for short swing link-fitted stock to be used, avoiding any possible infringement of safety space of bogie equipment in close proximity to the live rail. On 12 September 1992, No 43098 passes Millbrook, near Southampton, trailing the 06.18 Manchester-Bournemouth. *CJM*

Left: Non-electrified West Coast services to Holyhead via the North Wales line were converted to HST operation in the 1990s, with Western Region and later Virgin stock used. On 5 September 1997, power cars Nos 43164/029 pass Penmaenmawr with the 09.00 Holyhead-Euston. *Russell Ayre*

Above: The Great Western Trains ivory, green and yellow livery adopted in 1996 looked very impressive on a full HST formation, but problems always existed in keeping stock clean. An immaculate all Great Western-liveried set passes Silverton, near Exeter, on 11 April 1997 formed with power cars Nos 43137 and 43196 following a naming event at Newton Abbot. *CJM*

Below: The original First Great Western or 'fag packet' livery was applied following transfer of the Great Western franchise to FirstGroup. A full green, white and gold liveried set, headed by power car No 43170 *Edward Paxman,* passes near Foxhall Junction on 21 May 2001 forming the 12.45 Paddington-Bristol Temple Meads service. *Brian Morrison*

Above: Laira depot's flagship power car No 43179 *Pride of Laira* makes typical light work of the stiff incline of Dainton Bank as it approaches Stoneycombe, between Newton Abbot and Totnes, with the 08.30 Paddington to Plymouth service on 4 May 2002. *Russell Ayre*

Below: The Scottish Highlands always offer some excellent photographic viewpoints, with mountains, bridges and open landscapes. For much of the winter, the area is snow-covered, rendering some excellent photographic possibilities. On 4 February 2003, a full GNER-liveried set is seen near Gleneagles while forming the Inverness-King's Cross 'Highland Chieftain' service. *Ian Lothian*

Right: GNER-liveried power car
No 43110, now named *Stirlingshire*,
heads the 07.55 Inverness to London
King's Cross southwards past Bardrill
Road, close to Gleneagles, on 6 August
2001. The GNER-allocated HST fleet
is allocated to Edinburgh Craigentinny
depot, but also receives maintenance at
Leeds Neville Hill and London Bounds
Green depots. *Russell Ayre*

Below: One of the prime photographic
locations for the East Coast main line is
around Colton Junction, south of York,
where the lines to Leeds and Doncaster
diverge. A suitable road bridge allows a
perfect view of trains and photography is
quite easy. Also slightly further south at
Appleton Roebuck is another good
location, where on 19 September 2005
power cars Nos 43117 and 43108 storm
past with the 15.55 Newcastle-King's
Cross service. *Richard Tuplin*

Above: In good lighting conditions, a full Virgin Trains red-liveried HST looked magnificent in the countryside. Here a full 2+7 formation, led by power car No 43157 with No 43088 bringing up the rear, passes Kettleside, north of Penrith on 31 July 2001 forming a Bournemouth-Edinburgh service. *Ian Lothian*

Below: Carrying the short-lived Virgin CrossCountry branding, and sporting a yellow cab roof, power car No 43093 leads the 09.30 Newquay-Edinburgh summer relief service down Wellington bank on 31 May 1997. The CrossCountry branding was applied to the first few power cars repainted in Virgin red, prior to the company being awarded the West Coast franchise, after which the entire operation was just branded 'Virgin'. *Russell Ayre*

Above: A line up of Virgin and Midland Mainline HSTs at Sheffield on 28 August 2002. The Virgin set on the left forming a Newcastle-Plymouth train has a buffer-fitted power car on the rear, while a full teal green, orange and tan Midland Mainline set awaits departure to London St Pancras. *CJM*

Right: The second or revised Midland Mainline livery for power cars is centred on a dark blue livery, off-set by white and grey 'blocks' and the Midland Mainline name and logo, with an orange base band. Power car No 43074 is illustrated. Note the revised front end light clusters. *CJM*

Left: Displaying full standard Virgin Trains livery, with a black cab roof, power car No 43104 is seen in the yard at Adtranz Crewe on 29 March 2001, following a major overhaul and return to traffic after a long period of storage. *CJM*

Above: FirstGroup's corporate colour of mid-blue was progressively applied to the HST fleet in the early 2000s. At first this consisted of a white flash on the cab side, but after a short while this was replaced by an all blue side, with just the pink 'flash' to break up the body line. Showing the original First Great Western blue livery, power car No 43165 leads the 11.06 Paddington-Newquay past Teignmouth boat yard on 28 September 2002. *CJM*

Below: Displaying the revised First Great Western livery, complete with 'First' branding on the nose end, and all-blue body sides, power car No 43016 *Peninsular Medical School* leads the 09.15 Paddington-Swansea past Undy between Newport and Cardiff on 30 May 2005. *Brian Morrison*

Above and Left: In the hope that FirstGroup will be awarded the Greater Western Franchise from mid-2006, a pair of trailer vehicles, Nos 40423 and 42353, were trial refurbished to demonstrate what the company will offer if the franchise is awarded to First. The exterior is finished in a 'First Transforming Travel' colour scheme and the interior of both first, standard and the buffer area is totally rebuilt. Standard seating is retained in a mix of airline and table groups in the 2+2 style, while first class uses the 2+1 layout. The demonstrator vehicles are seen on display in Swindon. *CJM*

What might have been

This is an artist's impression of what might have been carried by the proposed eight 2+5 'Virgin Challenger' sets, if the project had been given authorisation. Power cars would have been given a heavy overhaul and refurbishment, including a re-wire, revised cooler groups and improved cabs. However, the project was abandoned soon after launch of the Voyager fleet. This artist's impression shows a modified Voyager livery.

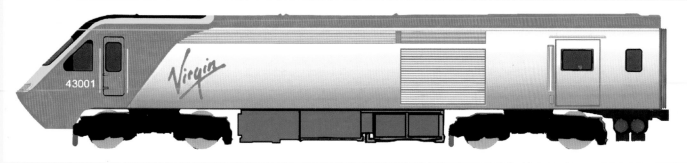

Two eras of high speed rail travel make a pass at Teignmouth, Devon, on 14 August 2004, with First Great Western power car No 43148 leading the 06.42 Penzance-Paddington, passing a Virgin Voyager set No 221114 forming a Newcastle-Plymouth service. Many people wonder if in 25-plus years' time we will still see the Voyager fleet operating the core high-speed diesel services in the UK. *CJM*